STARS OF HIP-HOP

KENDRICK LAMAR

STORYTELLER OF COMPTON

THERESE M. SHEA

Enslow Publishing
101 W. 23rd Street
Suite 240
New York, NY 10011
USA

enslow.com

Published in 2020 by Enslow Publishing, LLC.
101 W. 23rd Street, Suite 240, New York, NY 10011

Library of Congress Cataloging-in-Publication Data

Names: Shea, Therese M., author.
Title: Kendrick Lamar : storyteller of Compton / Therese M. Shea.
Description: New York : Enslow Publishing, 2020. | Series: Stars of hip-hop |
Audience: Grade 2. | Includes bibliographical references and index.
Identifiers: LCCN 2018044063 | ISBN 9781978509597 (library bound) | ISBN
9781978510289 (pbk.) | ISBN 9781978510302 (6 pack)
Subjects: LCSH: Lamar, Kendrick, 1987—Juvenile literature. | Rap musicians—
United States—Biography—Juvenile literature.
Classification: LCC ML3930.L136 S55 2020 | DDC 782.421649092 [B] —dc23
LC record available at https://lccn.loc.gov/2018044063

Printed in the United States of America

To Our Readers: We have done our best to make sure all websites in this book were active and appropriate when we went to press. However, the author and the publisher have no control over and assume no liability for the material available on those websites or on any websites they may link to. Any comments or suggestions can be sent by email to customerservice@enslow.com.

Photo Credits: Cover, p. 1 Kevin Mazur/Getty Images; p. 5 Frazer Harrison/Getty Images; p. 7 AB1/Adriana M. Barraza/WENN/Newscom; p. 8 Noel Vasquez/GC Images/Getty Images; p. 11 Chelsea Lauren/WireImage/Getty Images; p. 13 Jim Spellman/WireImage/Getty Images; p. 14 Christopher Polk/Getty Images; p. 17 Joey Foley/Getty Images; p. 19 Johnny Nunez/Getty Images; p. 20 Kevork Djansezian/ Getty Images; p. 23 Kevin Mazur/Getty Images; p. 25 © AP Images; p. 26 Emma McIntyre/Getty Images.

CONTENTS

1 A KID IN COMPTON 4

2 INTO THE INDUSTRY 10

3 THE GOOD KID GETS BETTER 16

4 AT THE TOP OF THE GAME 22

TIMELINE 28

CHAPTER NOTES 29

WORDS TO KNOW 31

LEARN MORE 32

INDEX 32

A KID IN COMPTON

Kendrick Lamar Duckworth is better known as the rapper Kendrick Lamar. He was born June 17, 1987, in Compton, California. He tells powerful stories about Compton and his life through his music. Many think he's one of the greatest living rappers.

Kendrick's parents moved to Compton from Chicago, Illinois. They were trying to escape the gangs there. However,

Compton has gangs, too. His parents tried
to keep him away from the fighting. They
kept him busy with activities. He loved
to play basketball with his friends. But
Kendrick was always watching the people
around him.

A TALENTED WRITER

Kendrick was a good student. "School was pretty fun for me," he said.[1] His parents and teachers encouraged him. He was good at writing. He even read the dictionary. He learned in English class that he had a gift for writing.

A teacher got him into poetry in seventh grade. He used what he learned to write

Early Influences

Young Kendrick listened to rappers such as Snoop Dogg and Jay-Z. He also saw Dr. Dre and Tupac Shakur shoot a music video. "It sparked something," he said. "I always kept thinking about that moment."[2]

rap **lyrics**. "You could put all your feelings down on a sheet of paper, and they'd make sense to you," he said. "I liked that."[3]

Many of Kendrick's friends were in gangs. He almost joined a gang, too. "That's when I knew something else had to happen," he said.[4] Kendrick's music saved him.

Kendrick Lamar's mother, Paula Oliver, attends the 2016 BET Awards. She supported her son's dreams.

GETTING A RECORD DEAL

By sixteen years old, Kendrick was using the rap name K.Dot. He had been rapping for eight years. In 2003, he put out a **mixtape** of his music. It was called *Y.H.N.I.C.*

Anthony Tiffith (*left*) and Kendrick Lamar hang out at a basketball game in Los Angeles, California, in 2015.

A friend told Kendrick to perform for Anthony "Top Dawg" Tiffith. Tiffith was the owner of a **record label**. Kendrick rapped for two hours. Tiffith said, "What impressed me was how **advanced** Kendrick was at 16 years old."[5] Tiffith offered Kendrick a record deal.

"That's when I knew something else had to happen."

INTO THE INDUSTRY

Working with a record label helped Kendrick Lamar. In 2005, he **released** a mixtape called *Training Day*. He performed with the rapper The Game. Lamar also worked with Lil Wayne. Lamar released a mixtape called *C4* in 2009. That same year, Lamar became part of the rap group Black Hippy.

Lamar dropped the name K.Dot. He started rapping as Kendrick Lamar. His friends still call him "Dot."

Kendrick Lamar and The Game (*right*) perform together in 2015.

The album called *The Kendrick Lamar EP* came out in 2009. It was his first album with a record label.

"DESTINED FOR GREATNESS"

In 2010, Kendrick Lamar put out a mixtape called *Overly Dedicated*. He rapped about the city of Compton. Famous **producer** Dr. Dre heard one of the songs. It was called "**Ignorance** Is Bliss." He loved the song. Lamar explained why. "It gave him both sides of the story in Compton, the **victim** and the **aggressor**," he said.[1]

Dr. Dre said, "You just knew this guy was **destined** for

"It gave him both sides of the story in Compton, the victim and the aggressor."

Dr. Dre

Dr. Dre's real name is André Romelle Young. He was one of the first people to do gangsta rap. This is a style that talks about street life. In 1986, he started the group N.W.A. He later became a producer.

greatness."[2] Dr. Dre asked Lamar to work with his record label, Aftermath. They worked together on Lamar's next album.

EDUCATING BY ENTERTAINING

With Dr. Dre's help, Kendrick Lamar released the album *good kid, m.A.A.d city* in 2012. Lamar was the "good kid."

Dr. Dre (*left*) and Lamar pose at a Rock and Roll Hall of Fame ceremony in 2016.

Jay-Z (*left*), Pharrell Williams (*right*), and Kendrick Lamar attend the Grammy Awards in 2014.

Compton was the "mad" city. Lamar told more stories about Compton through his songs. He rapped about people, places, and events. He told the story of watching someone get shot. He had really seen this happen.

Lamar also spoke about the bad effects of drugs. Pharrell Williams was a producer on the album. He loved that Lamar could teach through music. Lamar was just describing his life growing up. People loved the album. It has sold more than 1.7 million copies.[3]

THE GOOD KID GETS BETTER

3

Kendrick Lamar went on tour in 2013. He traveled around the world. He went to more than fifty cities. He performed on TV shows such as *Saturday Night Live*. A short movie called *good kid, m.A.A.d city* was made. It was based on the album.

WRITING IT ALL DOWN

Lamar began to keep a diary. He said, "I didn't want to forget how I was feeling when my album dropped, or when I went back to Compton."[1] He filled several notebooks with his writings and drawings. He said these ideas made writing lyrics easy. His notebooks helped him with his next album.

Lamar waves to the audience in Cincinnati, Ohio, during the 2012 Under the Influence of Music tour.

GOING BACK HOME

Lamar worried fame would change him. He said, "The best thing I did was go back to the city of Compton."[2] He got to see the people he grew up with. He told them about his experiences around the world.

Lamar's neighbors loved how he told their stories through his music. He said, "They literally cried tears of joy when they listened to it."[3] Some people thought his neighbors were all drug dealers or killers. Lamar's music

> "They literally cried tears of joy when they listened to it."

showed them as real people. The people of Compton had struggles and dreams, too.

Lamar wants his music to be about truth. He wants others to learn to tell the truth of their own lives, too.

Lamar is honored with the key to his hometown of Compton in 2016.

Lamar accepts the Grammy for Best Rap Album in 2016.

BUTTERFLY FLIES HIGH

In 2015, Kendrick Lamar put out a new album. It was called *To Pimp a Butterfly*. This album didn't look back on his past. He rapped about being a young black man today. He talked about fame. He also

Kendrick Lamar and Tupac Shakur

Lamar looks up to rapper and actor Tupac Shakur, who died in 1996. He has a song called "Mortal Man." In it, Lamar asks Shakur questions. Shakur "answers" using old clips of his voice.

talked about **racism**. It won the Grammy Award for Best Rap Album in 2016. Lamar won the most Grammys of any artist that year.

In March 2016, Lamar released songs that hadn't been done in time for *To Pimp a Butterfly*. The album was called *untitled* **unmastered**. It was a huge hit, too.

AT THE TOP OF THE GAME

In 2017, Kendrick Lamar put out his fourth album. It was called *DAMN*. He said it was his best. The singer Rihanna and the band U2 sang on two songs.

A True Track

Lamar's favorite song on *DAMN.* is "DUCKWORTH." It is based on a real-life event that had happened to his father, Kenny Duckworth. He helped stop a robbery at a KFC restaurant.

The song "**HUMBLE**." became Lamar's first number-one hit as a solo artist.

Listening to the album from the first song to the last song tells a story. Listening to it from the last song to the first is a different tale. "Both of these pieces are who I am," Lamar said.[1]

The album topped the music charts. It won the 2018 Grammy for Best Rap Album.

THE FIRST PULITZER PRIZE-WINNING RAPPER

In 2018, Lamar was asked to produce a special album. It was for the movie *Black Panther*. He asked many artists to work on it. The album had different kinds of music, such as soul and house music. Lamar rapped on a few of the songs, too. The album topped the charts.

Then Lamar got big news. His album *DAMN.* had won the Pulitzer Prize for Music. The judges had listened to a hundred works. *DAMN.* was chosen because its songs told powerful stories about African Americans today. Lamar was the first rapper to win the Pulitzer Prize. It had been given to jazz or classical artists in the past. To many people, this meant hip-hop was a **valued** form of music.

Columbia University president Lee Bollinger shakes Lamar's hand. Lamar won the 2018 Pulitzer Prize for Music.

A FUTURE WITHOUT LIMITS

In 2018, Lamar got his first acting role in the TV series *Power*. He played a homeless man. He is at the top of the rap game. But

Lamar speaks during the 2016 MTV Movie Awards. He uses his fame to talk about important issues.

he is ready for new **challenges**. He might even go to college one day.

Lamar is focusing on his career for now. He returns to Compton to stay in touch with friends. He said, "I can't get rid of the 20 years of being with my homies, and knowing what they go through. I can't throw that away."[2] Telling their stories and his own will always be important to him.

> "I can't get rid of the 20 years of being with my homies, and knowing what they go through."

TIMELINE

1987 Kendrick Lamar Duckworth is born in Compton, California, on June 17.

2003 Lamar releases a mixtape called *Y.H.N.I.C.*

2005 Lamar releases the mixtape *Training Day*.

2009 He releases the mixtape *C4*.
The album *The Kendrick Lamar EP* comes out.

2010 Lamar releases the mixtape *Overly Dedicated*.

2012 Dr. Dre signs Lamar to his record label Aftermath.
The album *good kid, m.A.A.d city* is released.

2015 The album *To Pimp a Butterfly* is released.

2016 The album *untitled unmastered* debuts.

2017 Lamar releases the album *DAMN*.

2018 Lamar produces the soundtrack to the movie *Black Panther*.
Lamar wins the Pulitzer Prize for Music for *DAMN*.

CHAPTER NOTES

CHAPTER 1: A KID IN COMPTON

1. Andres Tardio, "Here's What Kendrick Lamar's Childhood Was Like," MTV News, July 6, 2015, http://www.mtv.com/news/2205410/kendrick-lamar-childhood.

2. Tom Barnes, "The Story Behind How Kendrick Lamar Became the King of West Coast Rap," Mic, May 27, 2015, https://mic.com/articles/119372/the-story-behind-how-kendrick-lamar-became-the-king-of-west-coast-rap#.MwW3eMweW.

3. Josh Eells, "The Trials of Kendrick Lamar," *Rolling Stone*, June 22, 2015, https://www.rollingstone.com/music/music-news/the-trials-of-kendrick-lamar-33057.

4. Lisa Robinson, "The Gospel According to Kendrick Lamar," *Vanity Fair*, June 28, 2018, https://www.vanityfair.com/style/2018/06/kendrick-lamar-cover-story.

5. Ibid.

CHAPTER 2: INTO THE INDUSTRY

1. Victoria Ahearn, "Kendrick Lamar Says Dr. Dre Was Drawn to His Fresh Approach to Gangsta Rap," *Canadian Press*, October 25, 2012, Questia, https://www.questia.com/newspaper/1P3-2800174081/kendrick-lamar-says-dr-dre-was-drawn-to-his-fresh.

2. Lisa Robinson, "The Gospel According to Kendrick Lamar," *Vanity Fair,* June 28, 2018, https://www.vanityfair.com/style/2018/06/kendrick-lamar-cover-story.

3. Keith Caulfield, "Kendrick Lamar Scores Third Million-Selling Album in U.S. with 'DAMN.'" *Billboard,* April 6, 2018, https://www.billboard.com/articles/columns/chart-beat/8295475/kendrick-lamar-damn-sells-million-copies.

CHAPTER 3: THE GOOD KID GETS BETTER

1. Josh Eells, "The Trials of Kendrick Lamar," *Rolling Stone,* June 22, 2015, https://www.rollingstone.com/music/music-news/the-trials-of-kendrick-lamar-33057.

2. Dave Chappelle, "Kendrick Lamar," *Interview,* July 12, 2017, https://www.interviewmagazine.com/music/kendrick-lamar-cover.

3. Lisa Robinson, "The Gospel According to Kendrick Lamar," *Vanity Fair,* June 28, 2018, https://www.vanityfair.com/style/2018/06/kendrick-lamar-cover-story.

CHAPTER 4: AT THE TOP OF THE GAME

1. Madeline Roth, "Kendrick Lamar Tells Us Why He Loves Playing *DAMN.* in Reverse," MTV News, August 24, 2017, http://www.mtv.com/news/3032281/kendrick-lamar-damn-reverse-interview.

2. Lisa Robinson, "The Gospel According to Kendrick Lamar," *Vanity Fair*, June 28, 2018, https://www.vanityfair.com/style/2018/06/kendrick-lamar-cover-story.

WORDS TO KNOW

advanced Mature for one's age.

aggressor A person who attacks another.

challenge A task that is hard to do.

destined Certain to be or do something.

humble Not full of oneself.

ignorance The state of not knowing about something.

lyrics The words of a song.

mixtape A group of recorded songs that is often given away for free in order to gain fans.

producer The person who is in charge of making and sometimes providing the money for a record.

racism Poor treatment of people because of their race.

record label A company that records and sells music.

release To make something ready for the public to use.

unmastered Not edited.

valued Highly respected.

victim A person who has been attacked.

LEARN MORE

BOOKS

Aswell, Sarah. *Kendrick Lamar: Rap Titan*. Minneapolis, MN: Essential Library, 2018.

Hill, Laban Carrick. *When the Beat Was Born: DJ Kool Herc and the Creation of Hip Hop*. New York, NY: Roaring Brook Press, 2018.

Morse, Eric. *What Is Hip-Hop?* La Jolla, CA: Black Sheep, 2017.

WEBSITES

Biography: Kendrick Lamar
www.biography.com/people/kendrick-lamar-21349281
Read more about the star's rise to fame.

Kendrick Lamar
www.kendricklamar.com
Check out news, tour info, photos, music, and videos on Lamar's official website.

INDEX

A
albums and mixtapes, 8, 10, 11–12, 13, 15, 16, 20–21, 22–23, 24

D
Dre, Dr. 6, 12–13
Duckworth, Kenny, 22

E
early life, 4–9

G
Grammy Awards, 21, 23

L
lyrics, writing, 6–7, 17

P
Pulitzer Prize, 24

R
as rap star, 16–21, 22–27